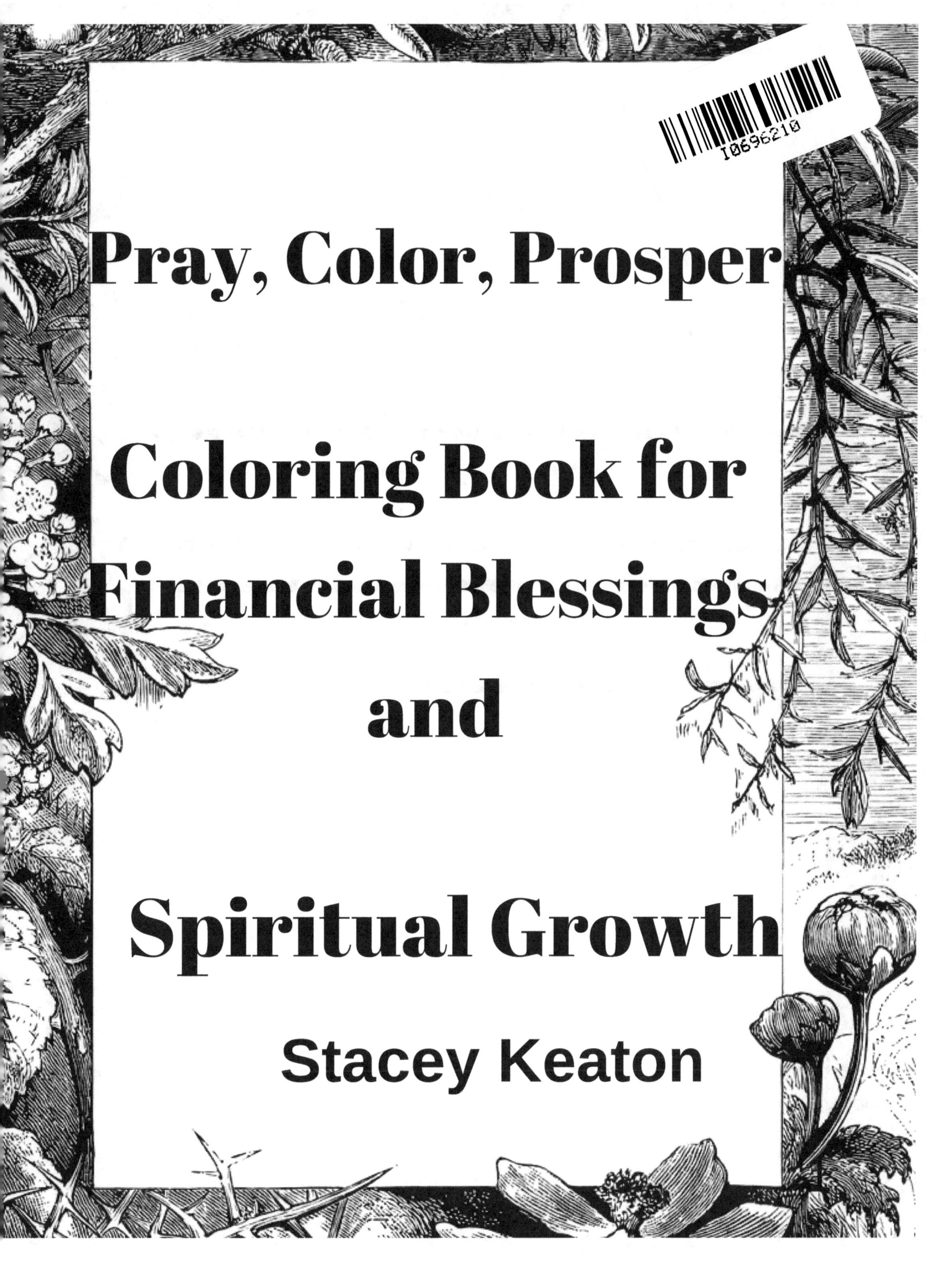

Pray, Color, Prosper

Coloring Book for Financial Blessings and Spiritual Growth

Stacey Keaton

This book belongs to

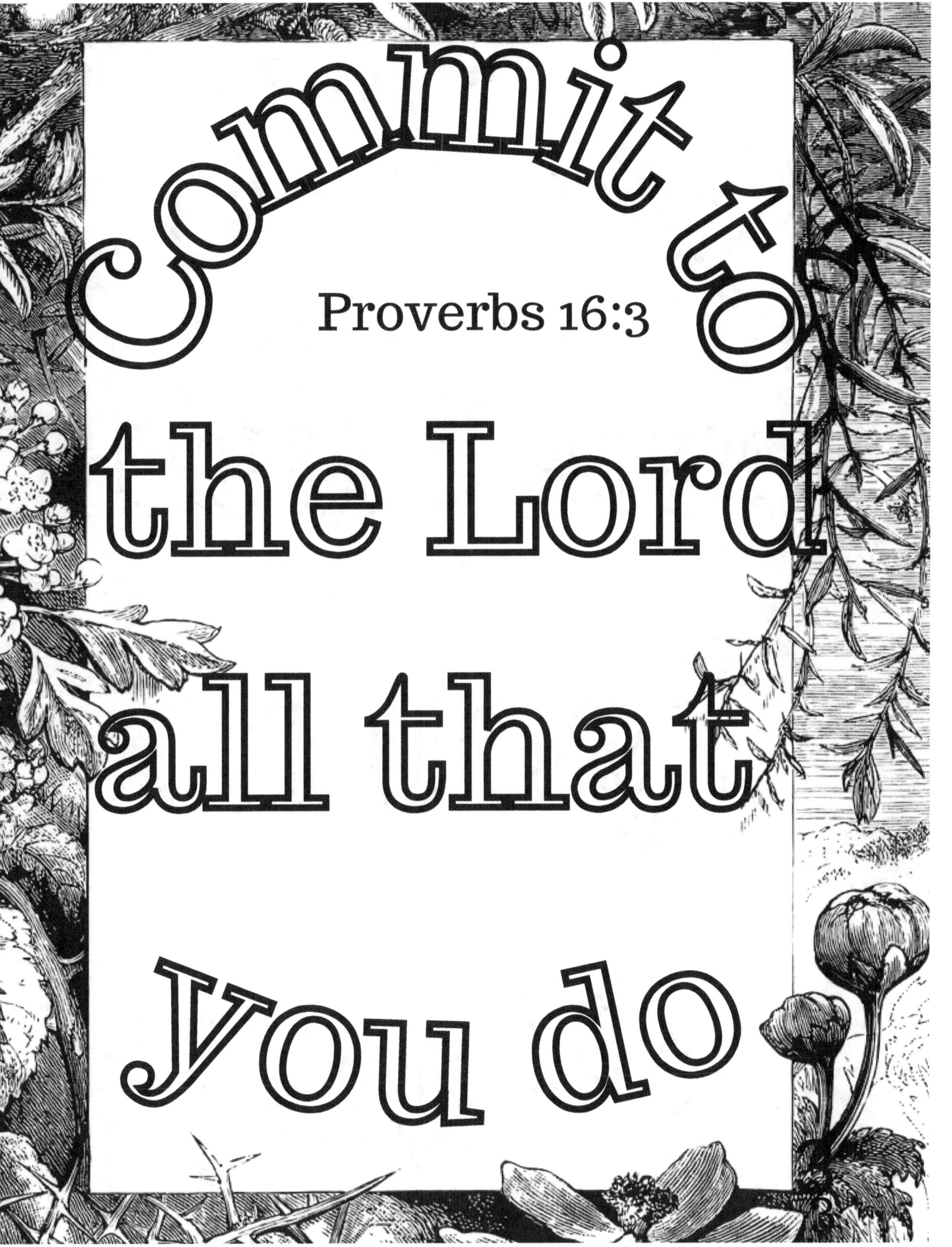
Commit to
the Lord
all that
you do
Proverbs 16:3

He will
Proverbs 16:3
establish
your
plans

Do you see
Proverbs 22: 29
a man
skillful
in his
work

He will
Proverbs 22: 29
stand
before
kings

and not
Proverbs 22: 29
stand
before
obscure
men

Invest in
Ecclesiastes 11:1-2
several
places
and
one of

these days
Ecclesiastes 11:1-2
you will
make
a
profit

The Lord
Proverbs 11:1
detests
dishonest
scales
but

accurate
Proverbs 11:1
weights
find
favor
with Him

Remember
Deutronomy8:18
the Lord
your God
for it is
He who

gives you
Deutronomy8:18
the
ability
to make
wealth

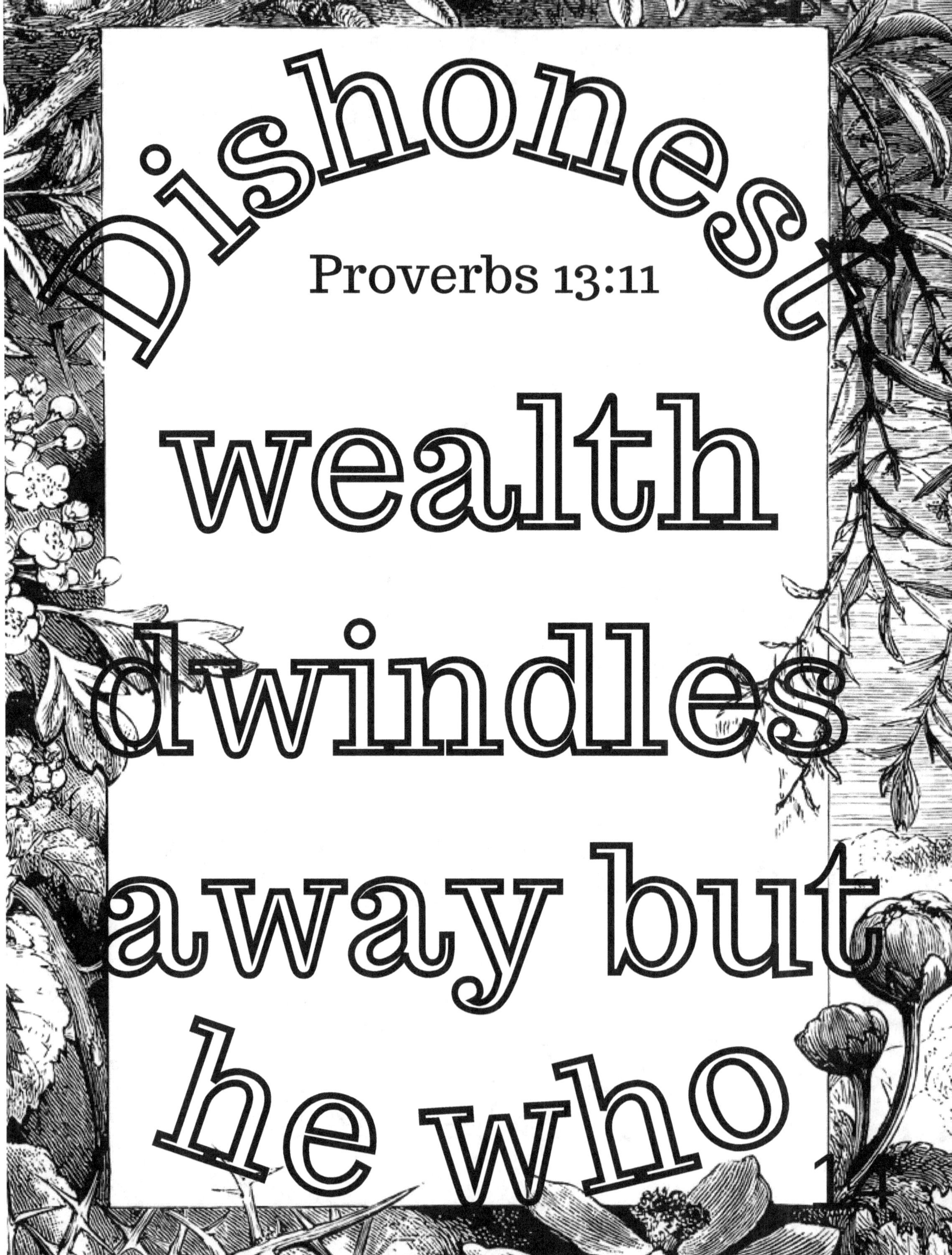

Dishonest
Proverbs 13:11
wealth
dwindles
away but
he who

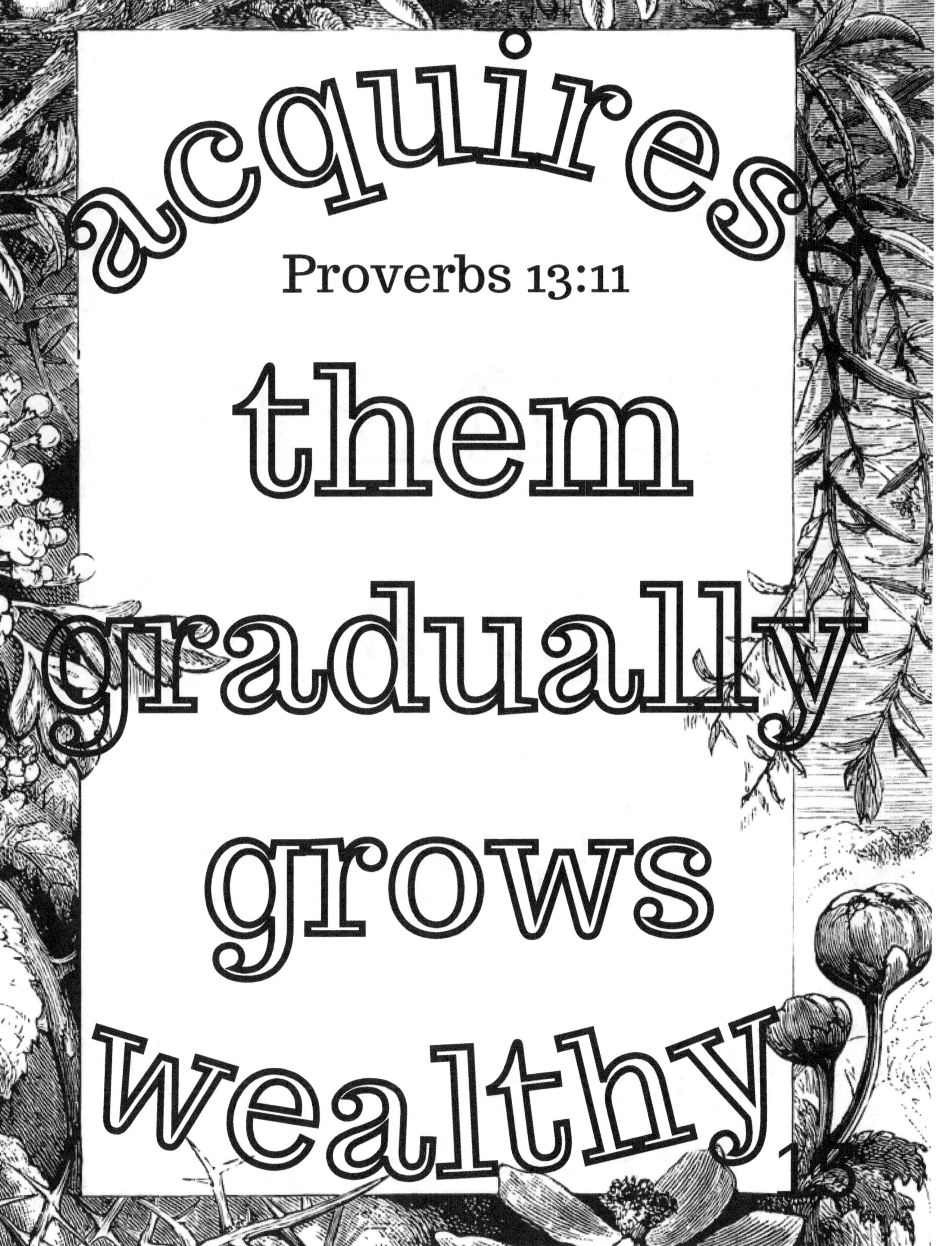
acquires
Proverbs 13:11
them
gradually
grows
wealthy

Proverbs 19:21

Many are the plans in a man's heart but

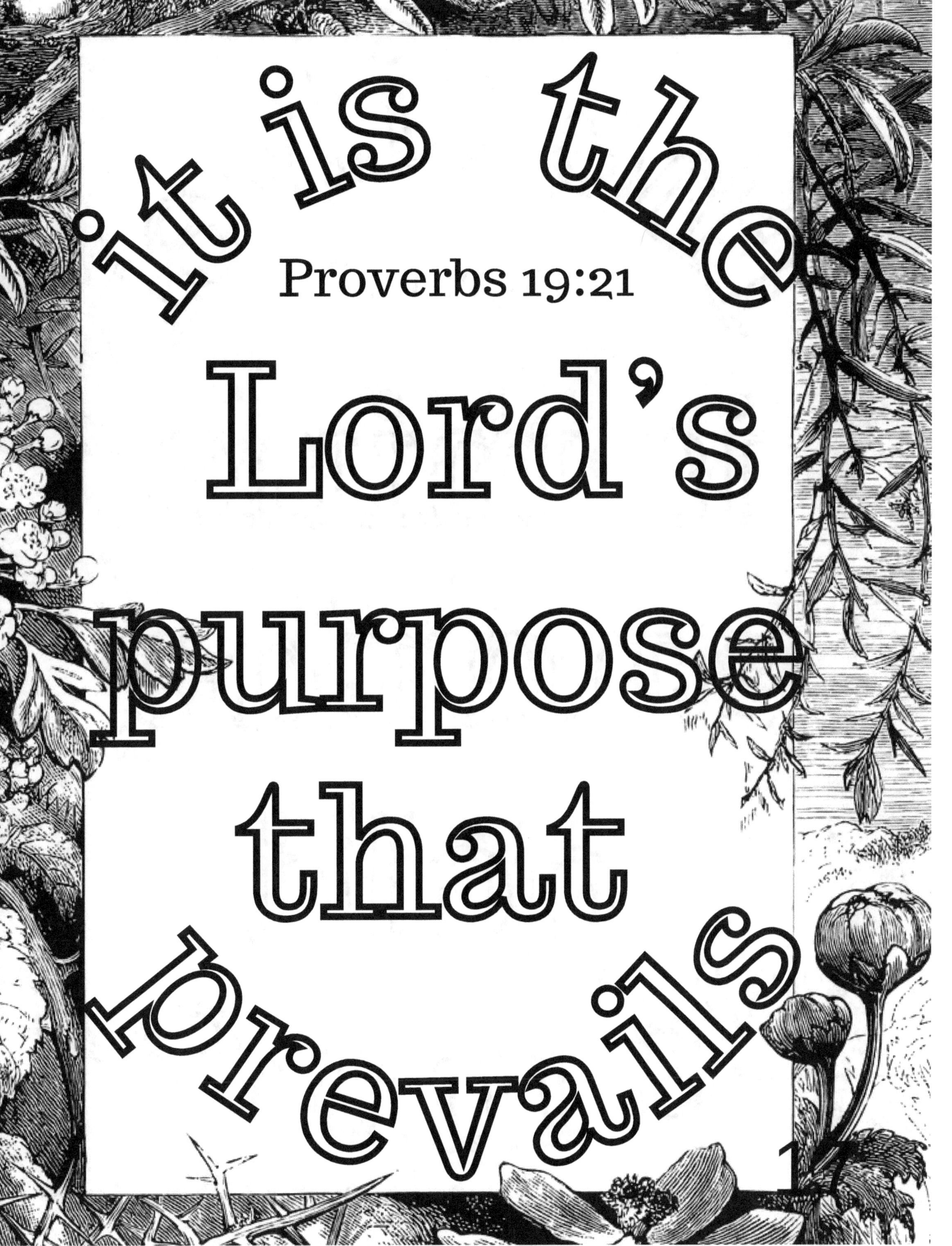
it is the
Proverbs 19:21
Lord's
purpose
that
prevails

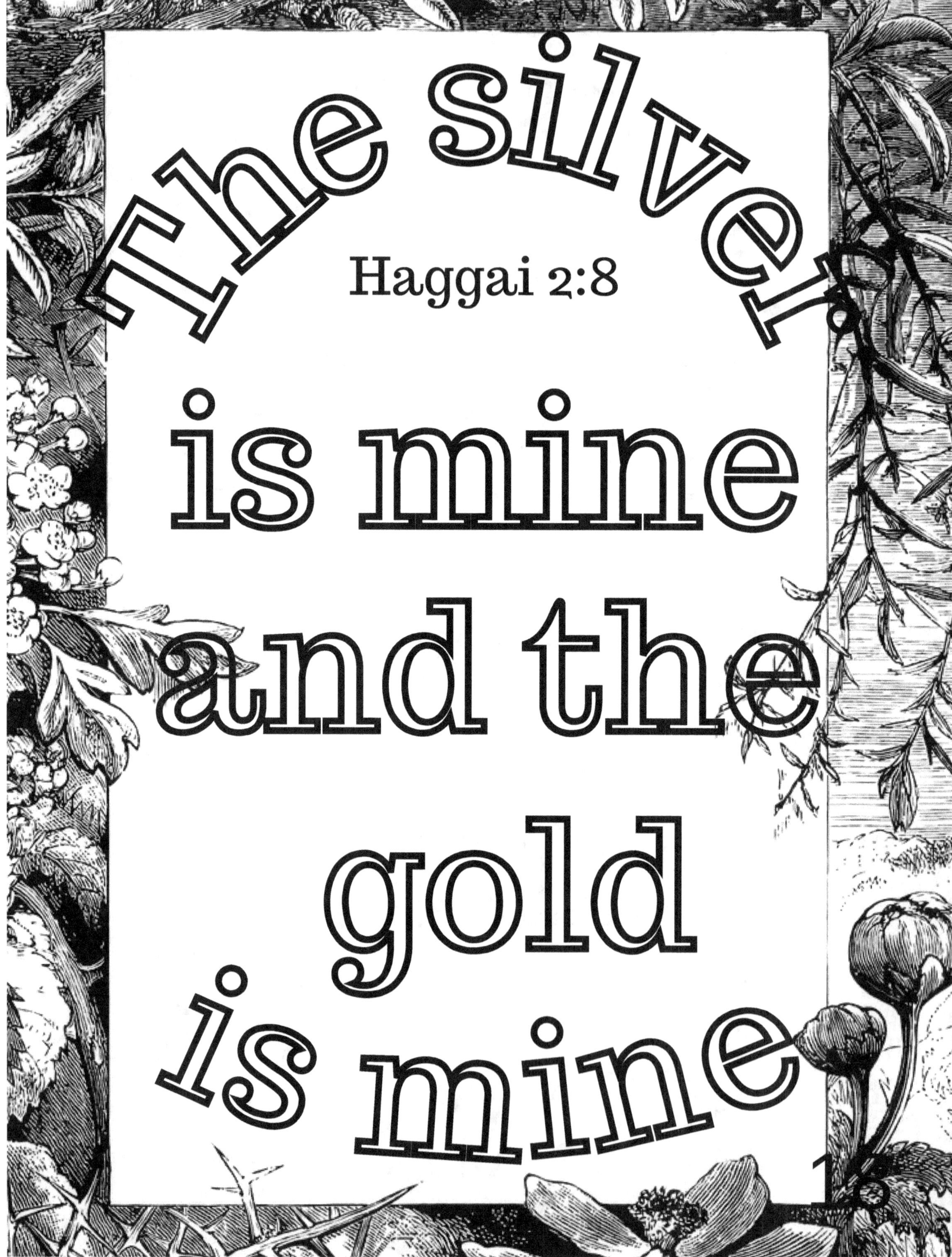

The silver
Haggai 2:8
is mine
and the
gold
is mine

says the
Haggai 2:8
Lord
of hosts

Both riches
1 Chronicles 29:12
and honour come from God

and He
1 Chronicles 29:12
rules
over
them all

Honor the
Lord with
your
wealth and
Proverbs 3:9-10

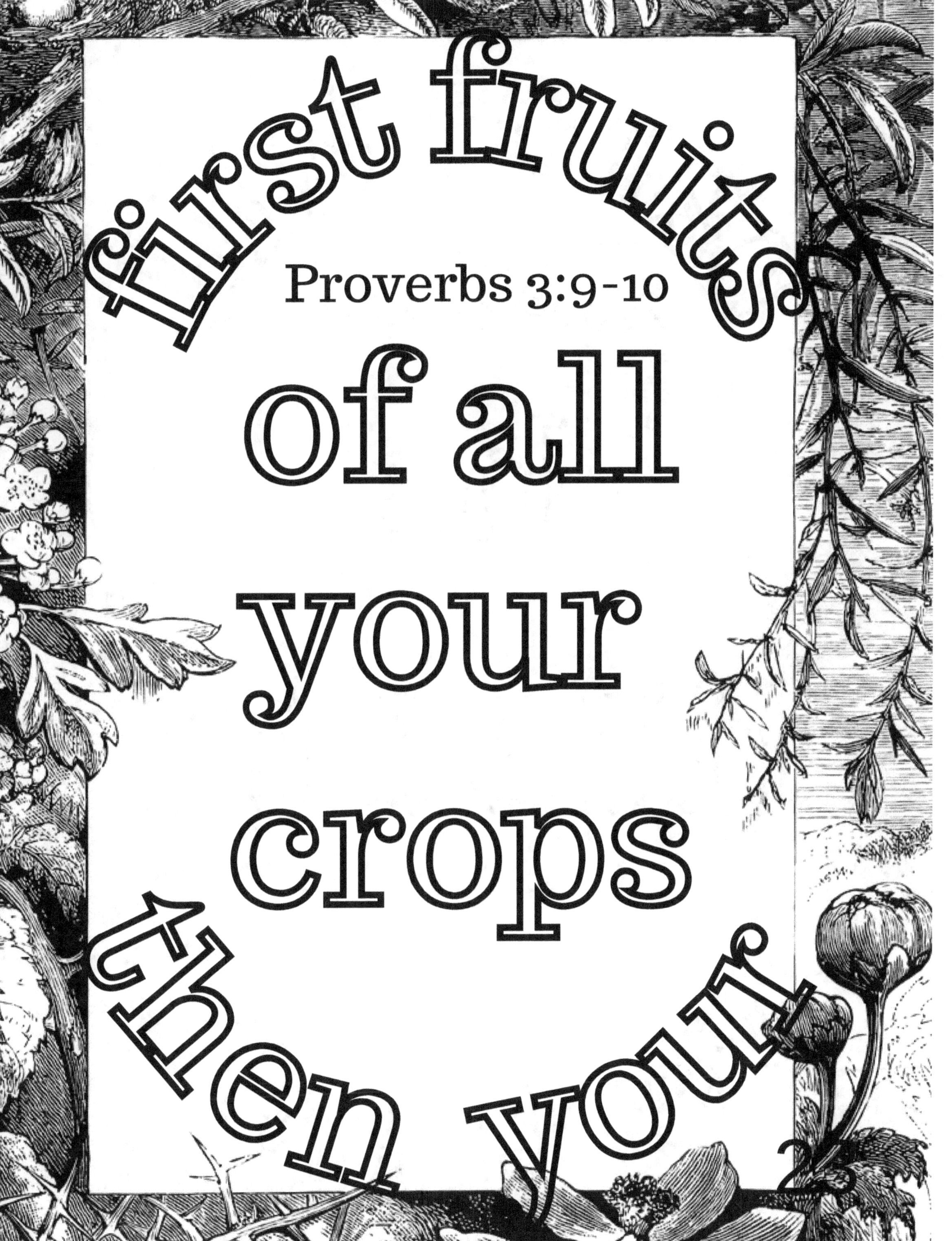

first fruits
Proverbs 3:9-10
of all
your
crops
then your

barns will
Proverbs 3:9-10
be
filled to
overflowing

If you
Job 36:11
obey and
serve Him
then you

will spend
Job 36:11
your days
in
prosperity.

Therefore
Luke 16:11
if you
have not
been
faithful

in the use

Luke 16:11

of

worldly

wealth

who will

28

trust
Luke 16:11
you with
true
wealth

With God
Proverbs 8:18
are
riches
and
honour

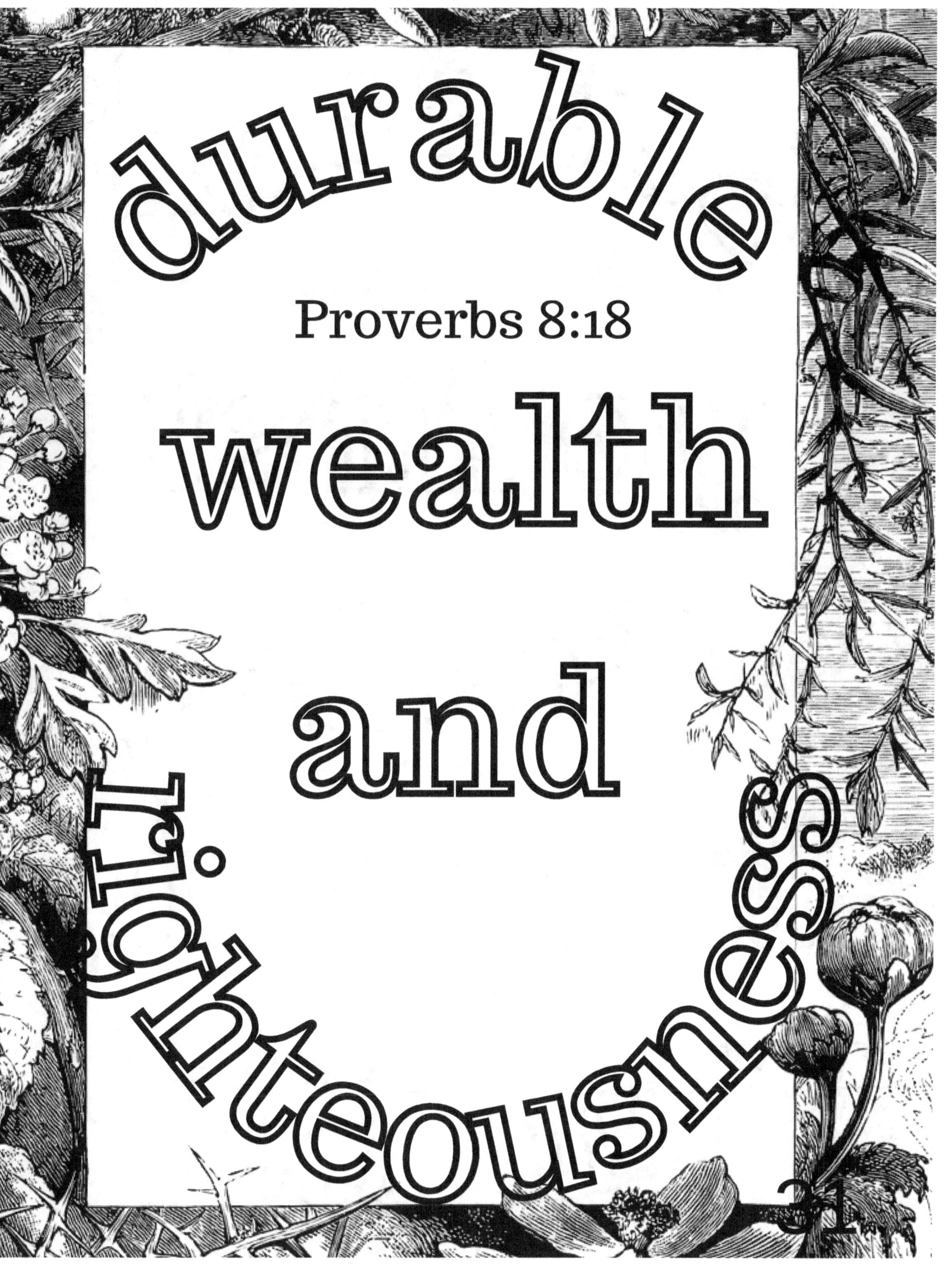

durable
Proverbs 8:18
wealth
and
righteousness

But seek

Matthew 6:33

ye first God's kingdom and His

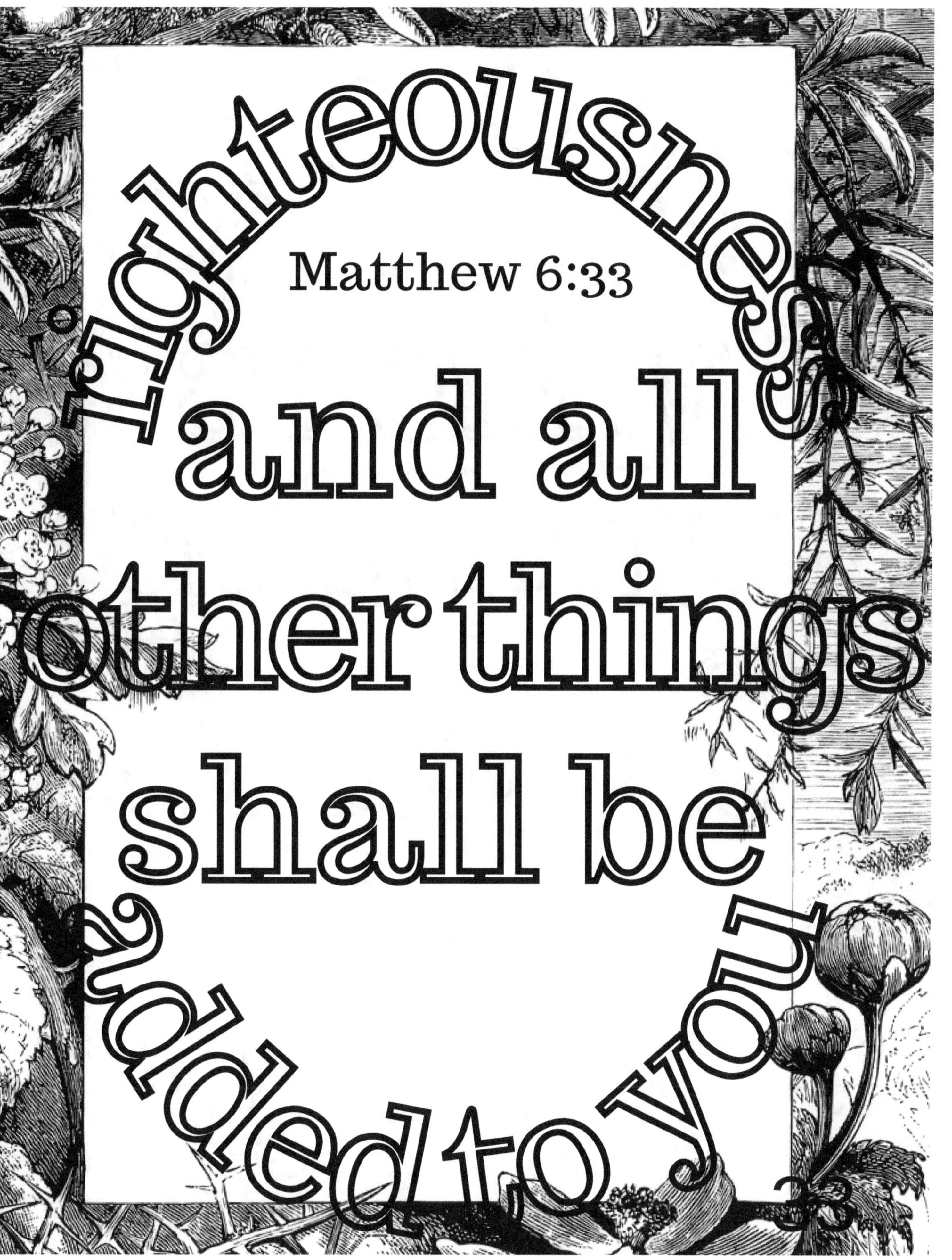

righteousness
Matthew 6:33
and all
other things
shall be
added to you

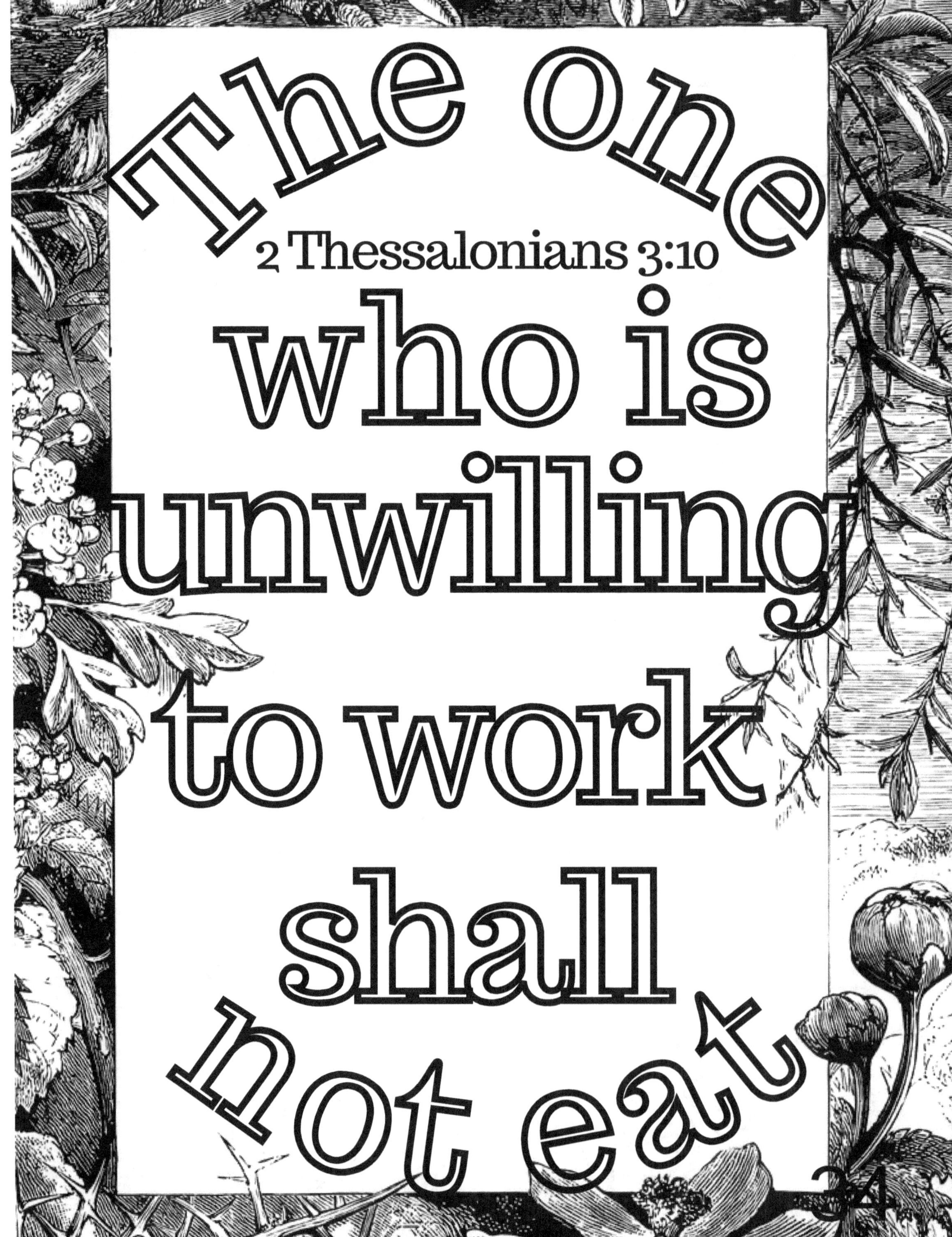
The one
2 Thessalonians 3:10
who is
unwilling
to work
shall
not eat

And God
Phillipians 4:19
will meet
all your
needs
according

to His
Phillipians 4:19
riches in
glory in
Christ Jesus

Keep your
Hebrews 13:5
lives free
from the
love
of money

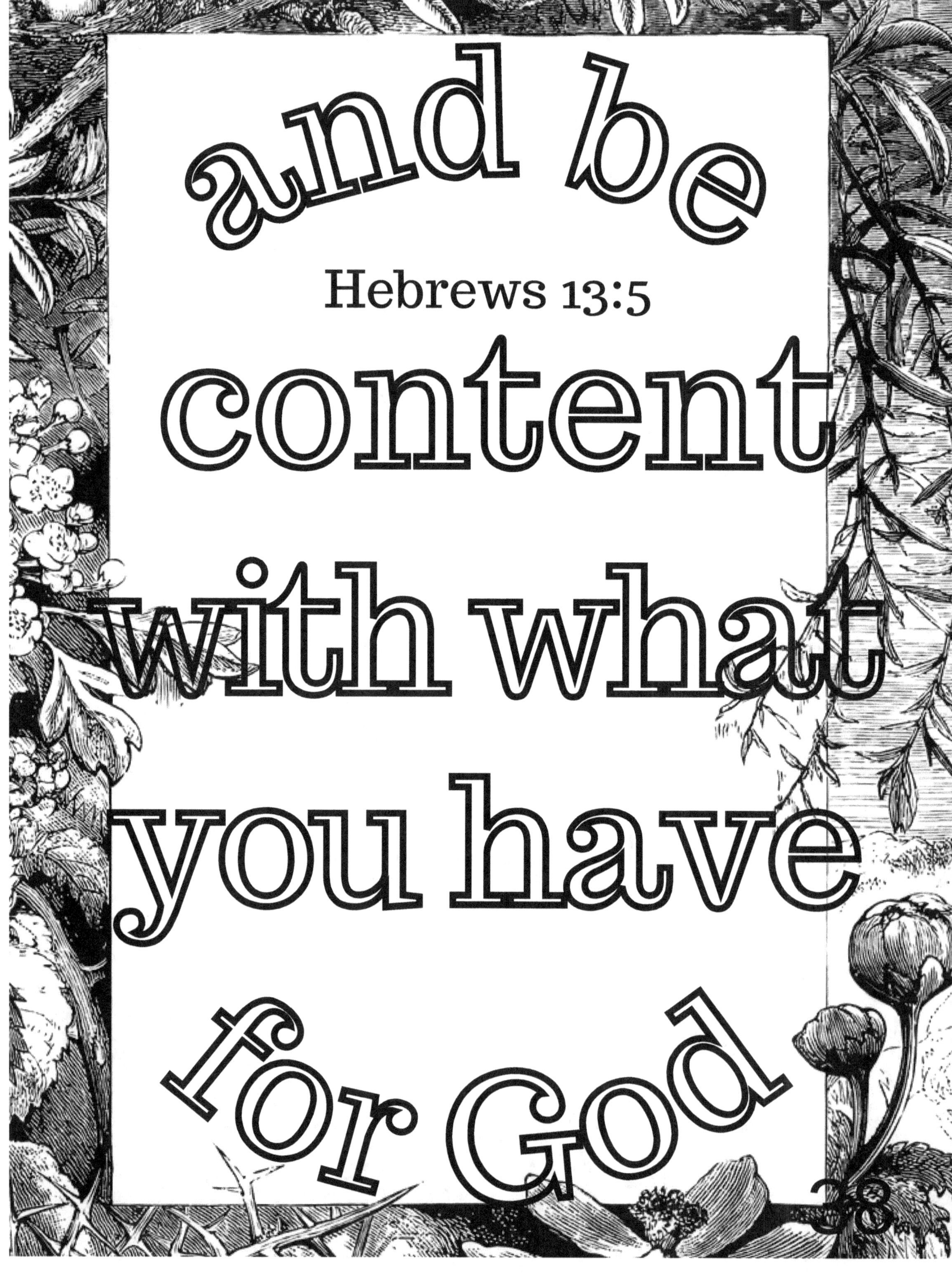
and be
Hebrews 13:5
content
with what
you have
for God

said 'I
Hebrews 13:5
will never
leave you
nor
forsake you'

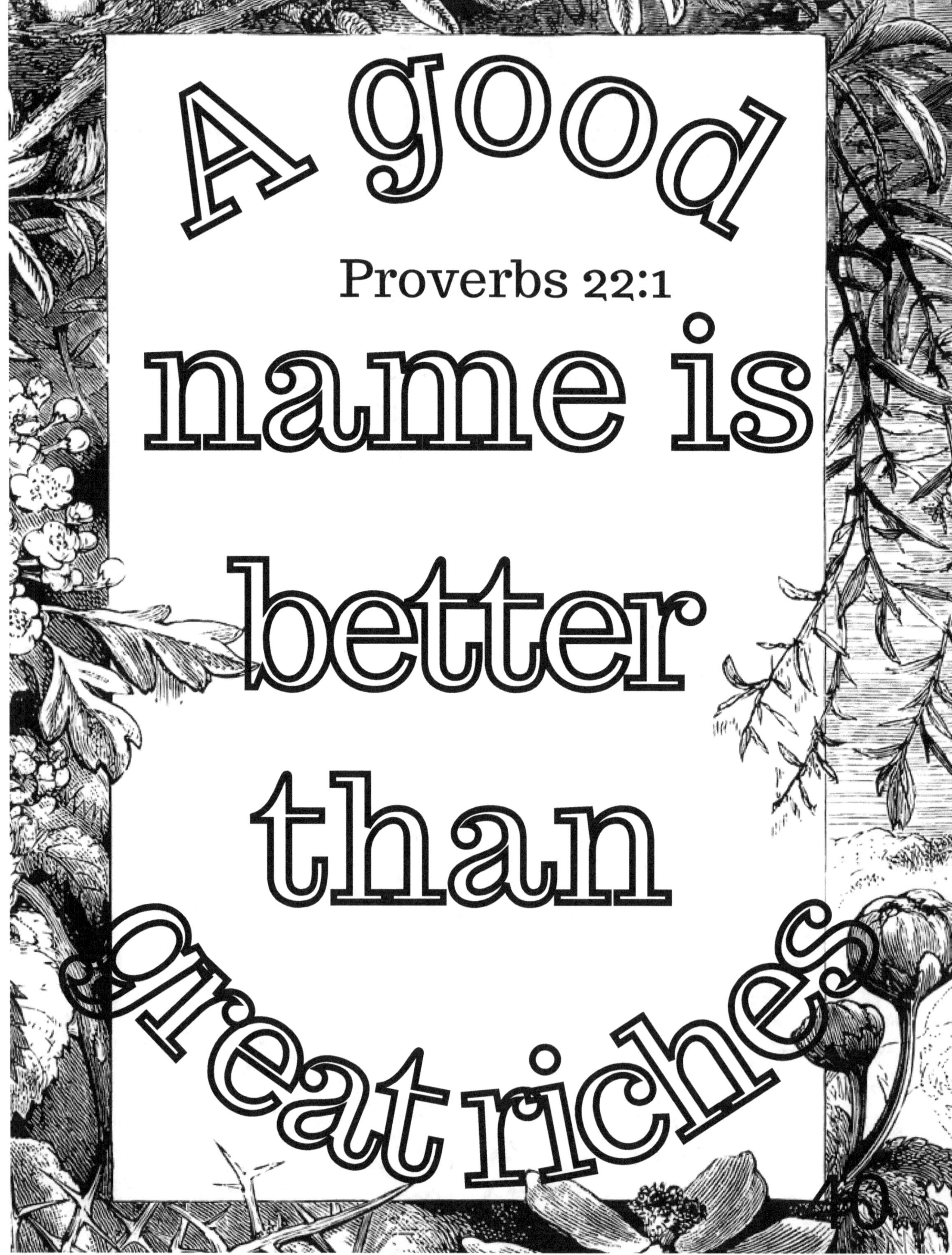
A good
Proverbs 22:1
name is
better
than
great riches

and favor
Proverbs 22:1
is better
than
silver
or gold

Lazy hands
Proverbs 10:4
bring
poverty
but
dilligent

hands
Proverbs 10:4
bring
wealth

I will
Isaiah 45:3
give you
hidden
treasures
and riches

stored in
Isaiah 45:3
secret
places
so that you
may know

that I am

Isaiah 45:3

the Lord

who calls

you

by name

You cannot
serve
both God
and money
Matthew 6:24

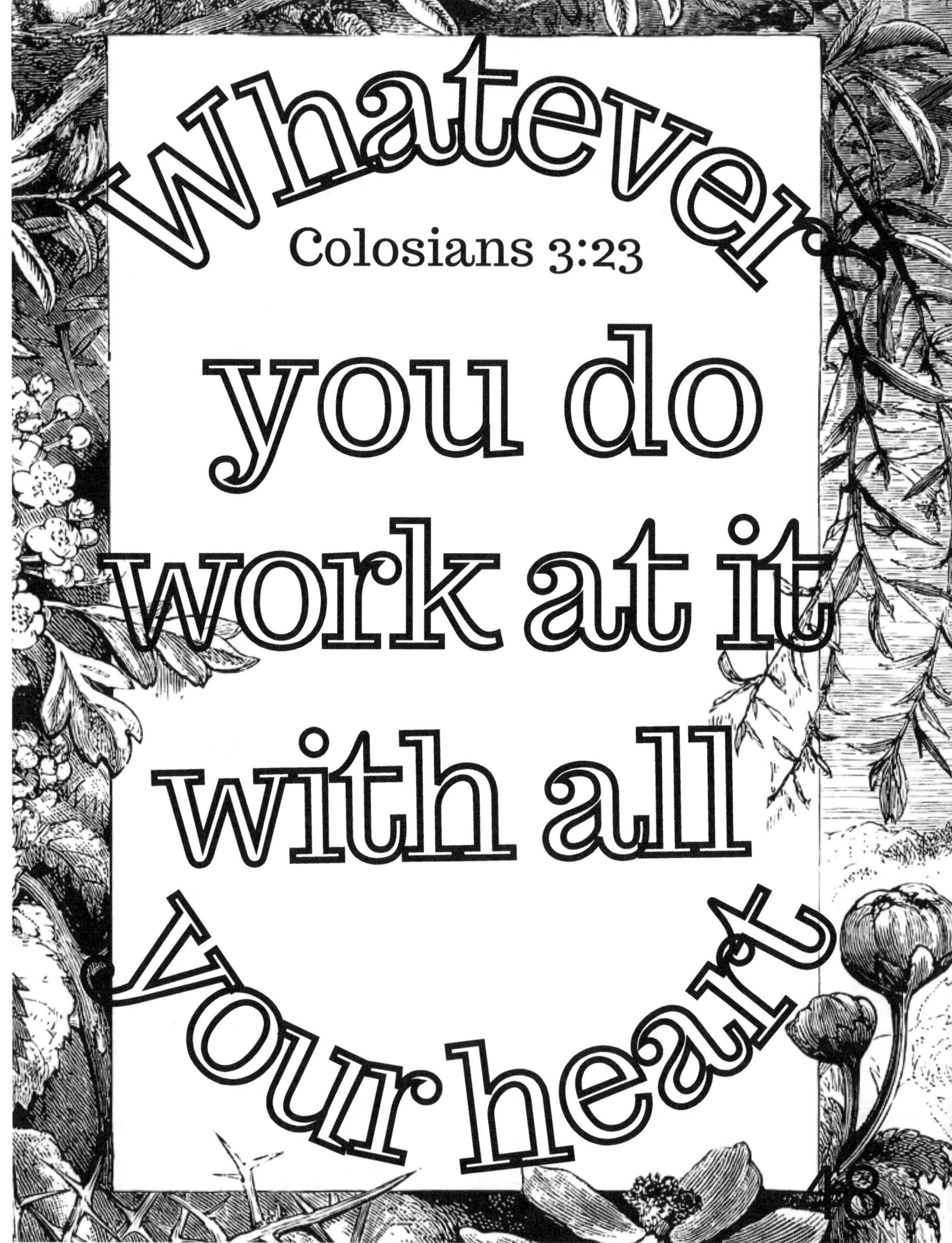

Whatever
Colosians 3:23
you do
work at it
with all
your heart

as working
Colosians 3:23
for the
Lord not
for human
masters

Don't extort

Luke 3:14

money and don't accuse people

falsely be
Luke 3:14
content
with
your pay

Better is
Psalm 37:16
the little
that a
righteous
man has

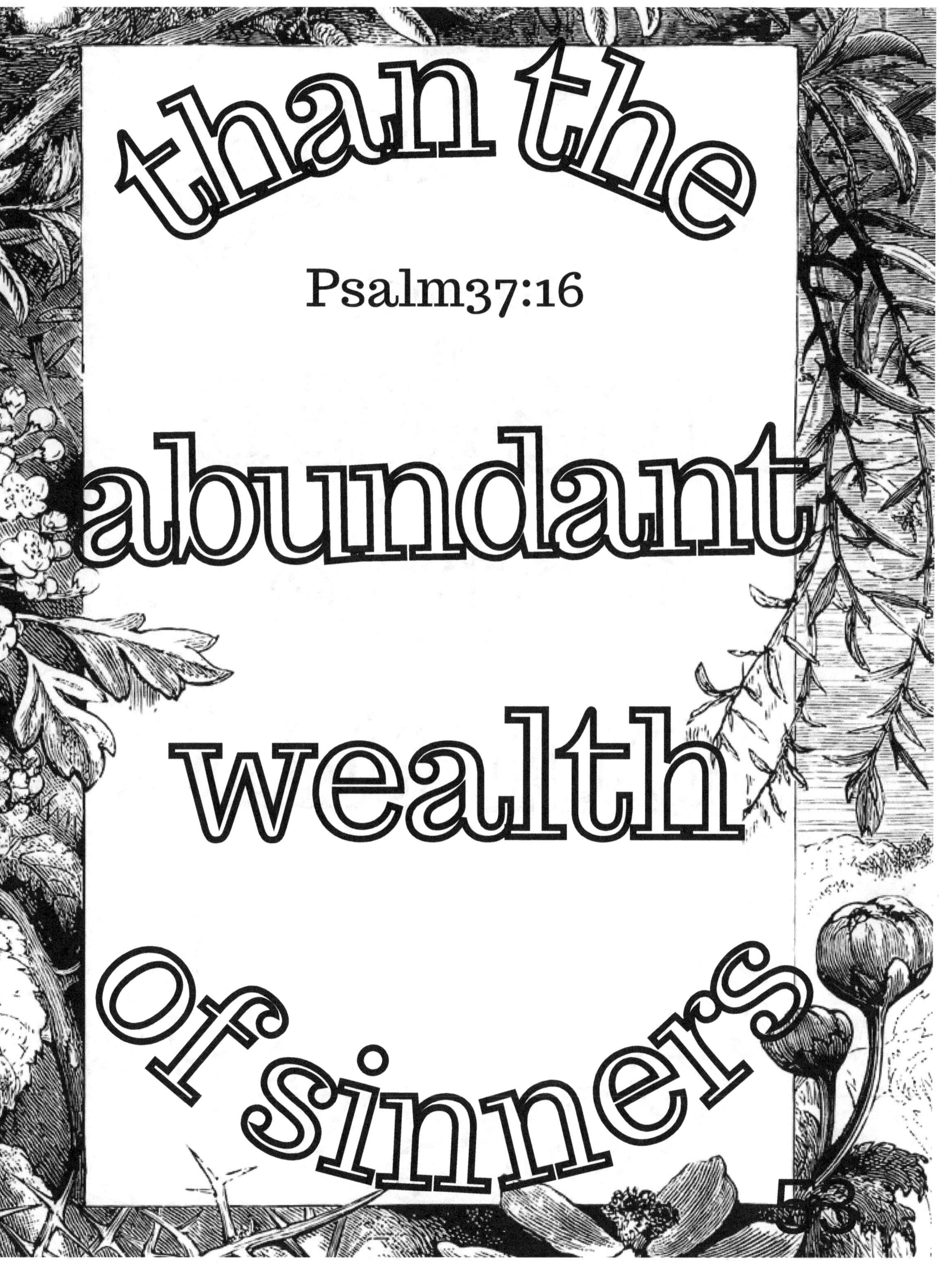

than the
Psalm37:16
abundant
wealth
of sinners

The Lord
1 Samuel 2:7
makes some poor and others rich

He brings
1 Samuel 2:7
some down
and lifts
some up

Better is
Proverbs 15:16
a little
with the
fear of
the Lord

than great
Proverbs 15:16
treasure
with
trouble

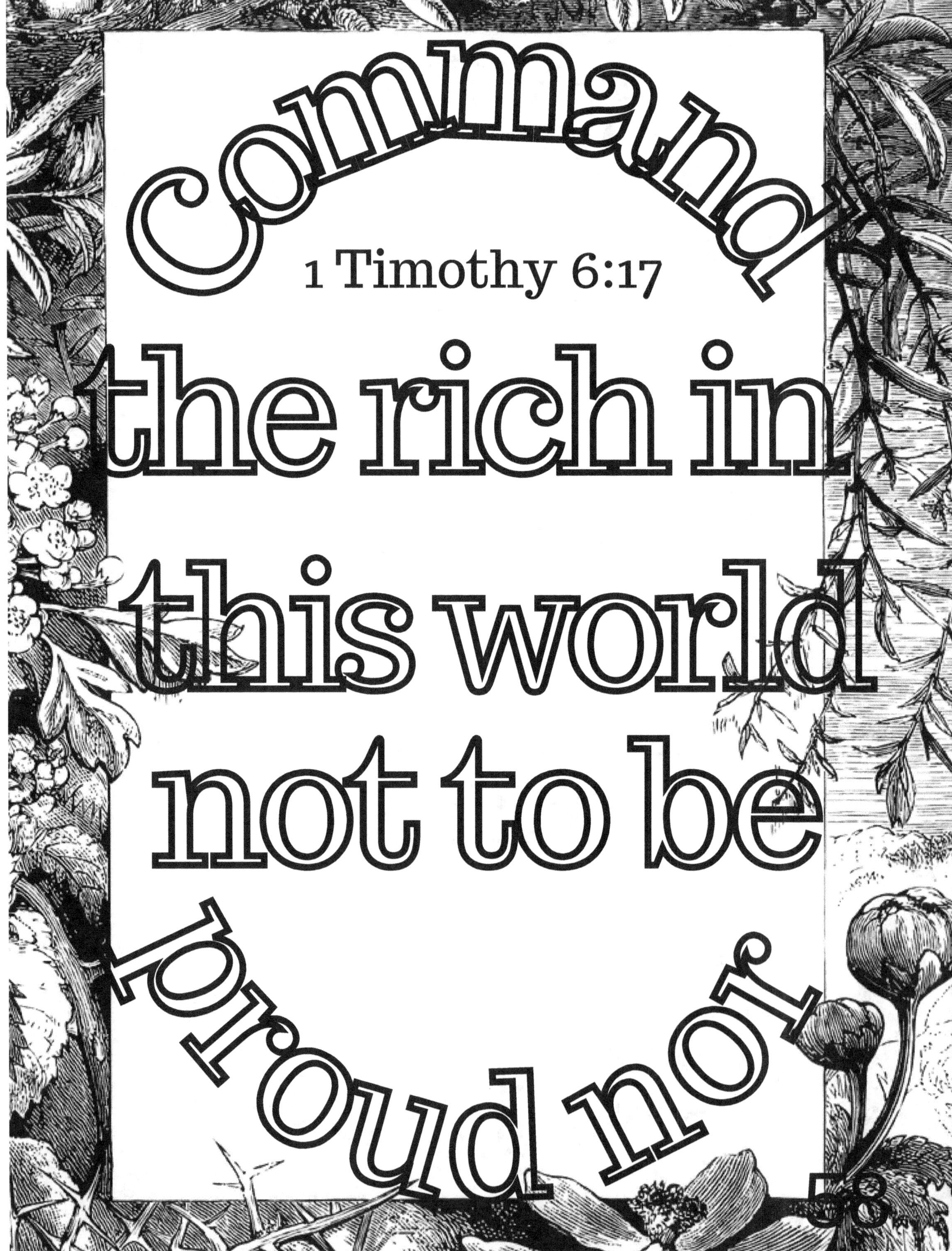
Command
1 Timothy 6:17
the rich in
this world
not to be
proud nor

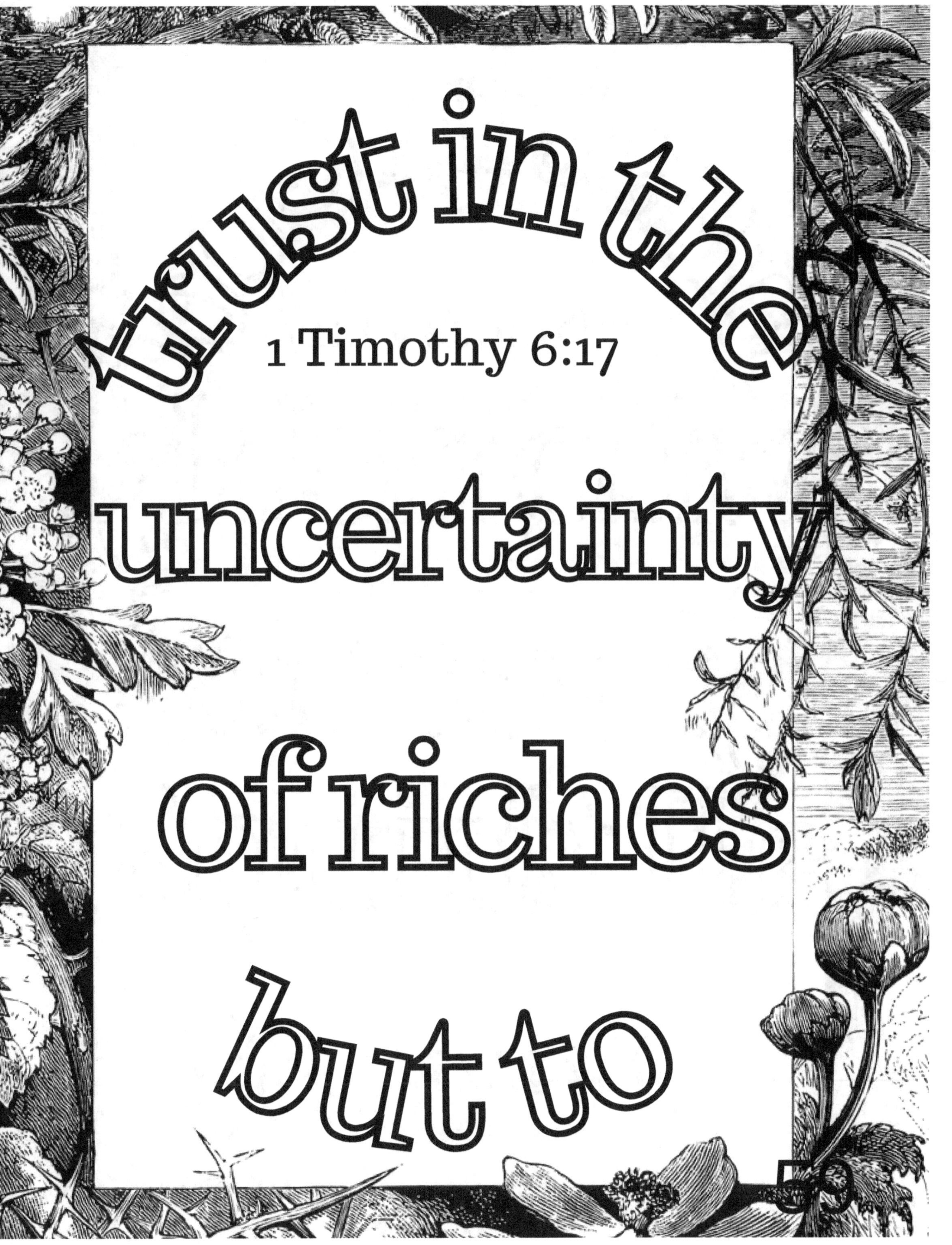
trust in the
1 Timothy 6:17
uncertainty
of riches
but to

trust in God
1 Timothy 6:17
who richly
gives us
all things
to enjoy

Command
1 Timothy 6:18
them to
do good,
to be rich
in good

deeds and

1 Timothy 6:18

to be generous and willing to share

The Lord
Deutronomy 28:12
will send
rain at
the proper
time from

His rich
Deutronomy 28:12
treasury
in the
heavens
and will

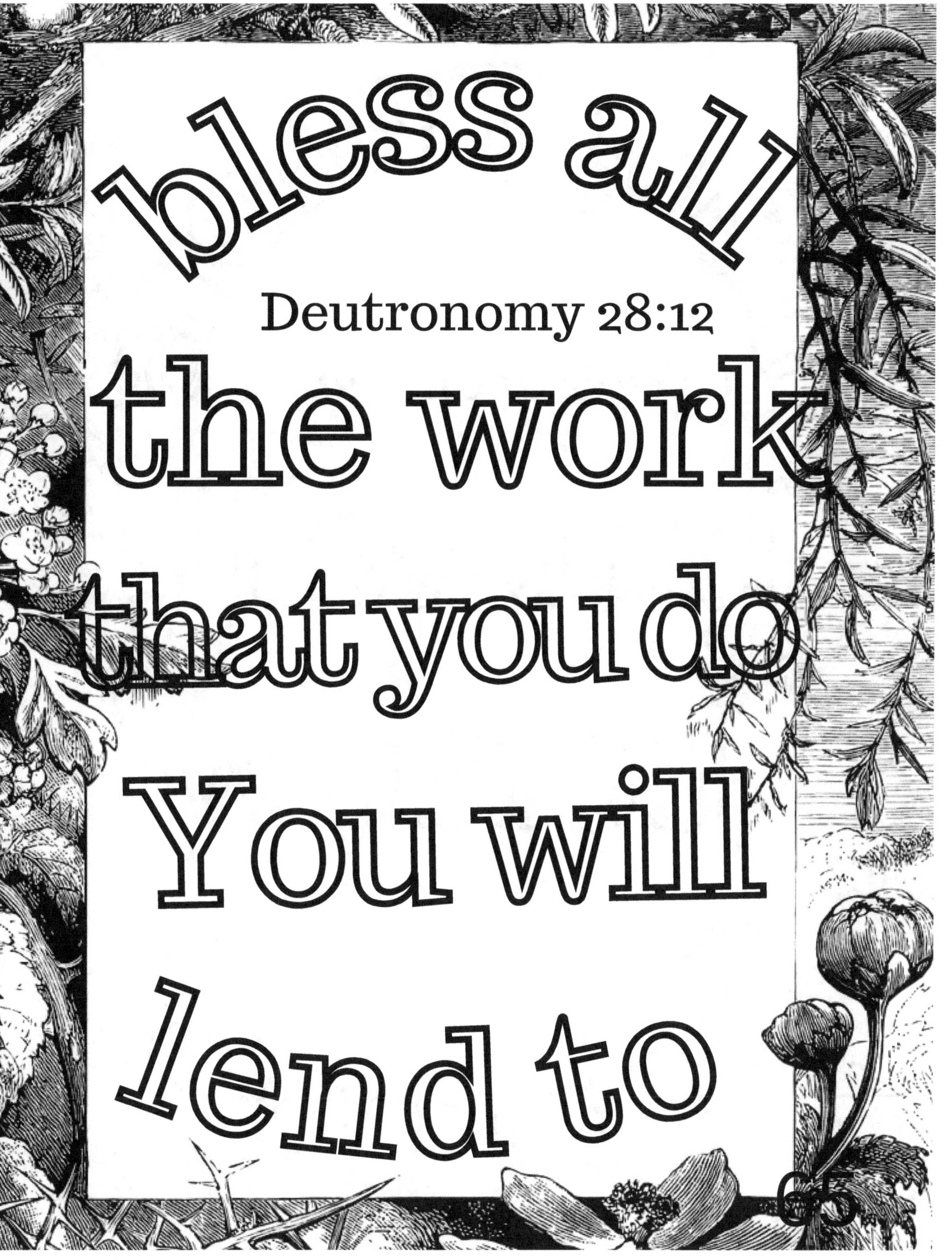

bless all
Deutronomy 28:12
the work
that you do
You will
lend to

many nations
Deutronomy 28:12
but will
borrow
from none

May the
Psalm 90:17
favour of
the Lord
our God
rest upon

us and

Psalm 90:17

establish

the work

of

our hands

Thank you
for
buying
this book